DEFEATING
ANXIETY

RALPH MOORE

A Straight Street Book

FOR

- *Eleanor Ruby, the girl God put in my life to insure that I get through it in one piece.*
- *Also for my faithful friends who stood with me during one of the most difficult stages of my life.*
- *Finally, for those people who continue to struggle under the weight of anxiety.*

RALPH MOORE

CONTENTS

RALPH MOORE

WHY YOU SHOULD READ THIS BOOK

If you are looking at this book I would imagine that you are probably in a good deal of emotional turmoil and pain.

I've written especially for Christ-followers who doubt their faith, or their *faithfulness*, because they are taking prescription meds for anxiety or depression. I also wrote for those who have rejected medication on the basis that it is not within God's will. And, I've met a few men along the way who refuse medication because they think it shows weakness and makes them less of a man to do so.

Some may have been "put down" by their pastor, church leaders or well-meaning friends. I know this because I was one of those pastors who *looked down* on people for taking drugs to alleviate anxiety or depression. My standard advice was, "Read the Bible more and kick up your prayer life."

Not bad advice…simply incomplete. And, I doled it out with little or no compassion. I honestly couldn't comprehend the struggles my friends experienced. God can and does heal marvelously. But sometimes things don't work out just as we pray that they will. When God doesn't answer in ways we hope for, we are forced to seek other options.

RALPH MOORE

.

1
WILL I EVER GET MY MIND BACK?

*The Lord is close to the brokenhearted; he
rescues those whose spirits are crushed. The
righteous person faces many troubles, but the
Lord comes to the rescue each time.*
Psalm 34:18-19

Several years ago I hit the wall…hard. I was
crushed by a panic/anxiety attack. It was the
most difficult period of my entire life.

Prolonged panic is difficult to describe
but *not* difficult to remember. People say that
if you suffer such an event you will never be

as afraid of anything else in your life as the fear of another such attack. What they say is true!

Problems, Problems, Problems

When I experienced acute anxiety, several problems climbed on top of each other to press me into a pile of blubbering flesh that couldn't talk without sobbing.

My wife was struggling through radiation and chemotherapy for breast cancer. I would rise at four o'clock most mornings to travel to the hospital with her. Having always been an eight or nine-hour-sleeper, the cancer treatments forced a lack of sleep which took a toll on me besides the incredible worry over my wife's health. Sleep deprivation aggravated a number of other fears as well.

The church that I pastor had stopped growing and was actually beginning a slow decline in numbers. I doubted my abilities to lead—wondering if God might be done with me.

The background noise included the loss of much of our savings in one of the drastic stock market downturns early in this century. Life looked pretty bleak. Finally, I experienced a very unusual set of car problems that created the actual breaking point for my emotions.

By the time I finally broke, I had already spent several weeks switching between various natural and "over-the-counter" sleeping medications in a vain attempt to rest my weary brain. I tried not to get hooked on any individual medicine, rotating between a half-dozen options trying for a simple night of rest. It seldom worked.

Not So Much Fun With A Hotrod...

The final straw began as a fun project. It was a hotrod. I traded a restored Corvette for a beautiful Jaguar convertible. Then the Jag suddenly needed a new engine. Two friends came to my rescue with a plan that promised a great deal of enjoyment. One friend would help me "juice up" a Chevrolet engine. After that, my other friend and I would swap engines in the Jaguar.

A Chevy engine in a Jag is a beautiful plan and something I had long dreamed about. It was already nice to take the Jag's top down in sunny Hawaii. The new engine would make the car spectacular.

The first friend owns a sophisticated machine shop—some of his products are flying on a NASA vehicle towards Pluto even as I write. He's also into fun. He carved out a section of his shop for playing with cars and motorcycles. He and I built the engine over the course of about ten weeks. I could only give two or three hours to the project each Saturday. Those days were bright spots in a pretty dark world.

After building the engine my other friend invited me to work alongside him while swapping engines in his auto-repair shop. So far so good…

I bought a really high quality (expensive) kit that matches Chevrolet parts to their

Jaguar mates. The Sunday afternoon after the kit arrived I stretched out on a sofa to read the instruction manual. The restful pursuit of a hobby suddenly turned to blackness and despair.

The manual cheerily informed me that two people could do the job in a single weekend of two *fourteen-hour* days. But I could only give a couple of hours a week to the project. That meant it would stretch into fourteen weeks of two-hour Saturday mornings. During that time I would have no car to drive. It also meant that my friend would push the car out of the shop each morning (can't drive without an engine) and push it back after work every evening. He has a small shop and would need to move the car, daily, just so he could run his business. You don't ask friends to do things like that—I freaked out.

No Sleep...At All

I stayed freaked out. It was so bad that I didn't sleep, *at all*, for three days and nights. After the third night my wife, who was still undergoing cancer treatment, called our family doctor about my condition. He was booked solid and his receptionist set an appointment for two days later.

I broke down and cried while my wife and the receptionist were still speaking. When I blubbered something about going to the emergency room our doctor got on the phone. He understood that I was really messed up. A half-hour later I was in his office.

Our doctor prescribed tranquilizers and they calmed me down about 45 minutes later. It felt great to simply feel normal. Though feeling very tired, there was no 'high' or 'low.' I just felt normal.

But it was a *different* normal. I felt fine as long as everything remained calm. However my mind was so fragile that we stopped watching television. The flashing images and loud commercials grossly unnerved me. My sweet wife bought a bunch of picture puzzles. We spent months quietly working on those puzzles before I gained enough emotional stamina to face television. My days of repeatedly switching between three news channels were definitely over.

But treatment didn't stop with the anxiety meds. My doc couldn't decide whether I was struggling with anxiety, depression or both. The initial medication was for anxiety and it worked. But in the meantime, my family doctor wanted to experiment with an anti-depressant. We tried the new medication after I had enjoyed two weeks of consistent peace and relatively restful sleep. The new drug made me crazy. I suddenly found myself overwhelmed by more anxiety than at the beginning of this sad saga.

Will I Ever Get My Mind Back?

I remember calling our doctor about four days before Easter. I was so shattered that I didn't think I could preach on Easter weekend. My friends had spent serious time praying for me, but I was still climbing the walls.

In addition to television, preaching was one of the few things that was difficult, even while I was on the original meds. But this new situation was worse than anything I had experienced to date. I was completely manic. I couldn't focus on anything for more than about 90 seconds. I was in no state to speak to a crowd of people, especially an Easter crowd.

I actually feared that I would end up like King Nebuchadnezzar in the Old Testament—if you remember he lost his mind for seven years. The Book of Daniel says that he,

> ...*ate grass and slept under the dew. He ate grass like a cow, and he was drenched with the dew of heaven. He lived this way until his hair was as long as eagles' feathers. (Daniel 4:33 NLT).*

Well, actually I didn't think I was as bad off as old Nebs, but I did think I would never have another completely normal thought in my lifetime.

Over the phone I asked the doctor, "Will I ever get my mind back?" His answer, "I can only tell you that 100 percent of people who get what you have get over it."

Those were comforting words. He then told me to stop the anti-depressant, which had triggered the additional anxiety. Two days later normalcy returned, although I was still taking the original meds for anxiety and television was definitely out of the picture.

Medicine As A Friend

I began to see the anxiety medication as a friend. And it is a friend to this day. At first I feared becoming addicted to it. Then found that addiction simply means that if you quit abruptly you will suffer anxiety—been there, done that.

I eventually changed doctors. The new doctor (a psychiatrist) doubled the anxiety meds and found something new to help me sleep. He later tapered the dosage back. His strong actions successfully overcame the terrible feelings. I even found myself able to cope with television. However we now mostly record TV shows and skip the commercials. The rapidly changing subject matter stills rattle my cage.

Along the way I discovered several tools for dealing with anxiety. They mostly involve simple decisions. Some are medical. Some are spiritual. Some involve plain old common sense. The good thing is that that they all work! However, they work best when used in *concert* with one another.

It often takes several influences, working together, to cause an overflow of adrenalin which propels anxiety, leading to the need for medication. In the same way, it takes several tools to keep adrenalin/anxiety in check. There is no "one shot fixes everything" option.

As I wrote in the introduction, I want to tip the scales towards medications because I've met so many people who feel guilt or suffer from condemnation for taking them.

Worse yet, there are those people who did take the meds, which soon made them feel better. Once they felt better, they assumed they were past their problems and didn't need the medications, so they quit taking them. People who do this often come to the somewhat confusing conclusion that the meds didn't work because they *stopped* working when they *stopped* taking them.

Whether you require medications, a re-treading of your spiritual tires or just a few lifestyle changes, you *can* get your anxiety under control. Victory will come your way. Read on and we'll look a little closer at what troubles you. And then we'll examine some tools that can help you live a great and balanced life.

2
REMOVING A CLOAK OF SHAME

So watch your step. Use your head. Make the most of every chance you get. These are desperate times!
(Ephesians 5:15-16 THE MESSAGE)

I still take the same pills that broke my initial anxiety nearly a decade into this experience. I take them because they work!

In fact I often *advertise* the fact that I am on medications. I do this because I've discovered so many people who wrap themselves in a cloak of shame for taking medications for anxiety and/or depression. I want to help set others free in any way that I can. I've found that talking about my own situation opens others to allow a little daylight into the shadowy corners of their lives.

As a result of my openness, nearly every month someone at church, or in the community, will come talk about their private (and often hidden) struggle with anxiety. My first approach is to describe my own journey through anxiety in an effort to help them feel less alone. Then I try to hook them up with the prayer team at our church—prayer works! The third step is to encourage people to seek medical attention as well as the help they receive from simply discussing their problems with trusted friends.

'Advertising' My Meds

About two years after my acute anxiety attack, I attended a conference with a select group of leaders from a church denomination. Each was a pastor and each also supervised several of other churches. They functioned as *both* pastors and bishops for the group. One speaker was Dr. Archibald Hart, who has written extensively on managing stress and anxiety from a Christian perspective. It was one of his books that gave me 'permission' to feel good about the pills that worked so well.

I left the room for a half-hour, during his talk, to record a short video. When I returned Dr. Hart was speaking about the value of medications in a Christian world that seemed to see taking them as a "spiritual failure." Walking back to my seat, I embarrassed myself with a spontaneous outburst that interrupted Dr. Hart's talk.

I held up my pillbox for all to see and shook it to make enough noise to attract attention. I then thanked Dr. Hart for his book, quoting the single paragraph that had freed me from my legalistic attitude toward medications.

I also confessed my prior disdain for people who needed pills for anxiety, even though I would *never* have criticized them for taking pills for a headache. Everyone laughed at what I said, leaving me to feel pretty foolish for the outburst. However, at the end of the morning session, everything changed…

Revealing Deep, Dark Secrets

It started in the men's room. One pastor (standing at the urinal) thanked me for speaking openly about my anxiety and the prescription drugs I was taking. He then said that no one but his wife knew he was on meds. He went on to explain how he feared that his denominational officials would fire him if they knew he was on meds (Don't forget these were the same officials who hired Dr. Hart to say that meds are OK). This man may as well have worn a jacket with the word 'shame' embroidered across the back.

As I left the restroom I discovered another pastor 'lurking' behind a pillar waiting for a chance to talk.

The second pastor also thanked me for what I had said in the meeting. I then told him about the astonishing conversation with the pastor who was afraid of losing his job.

The second pastor then told me that he was in the same situation as the first guy. But he was worse off—he was so bound by fear that he even hid his meds from his wife.

By the end of the day 19 leaders, out of 78 gathered there, communicated much the same thought. They spoke to me privately. They sent text messages. One guy even wrote a 'thank-you' on a napkin and passed it down the row where we were seated.

How Much Pain Is Out There?

There is much pain among Christian leaders. And it seems that 'cover-up' is the watchword among those suffering from anxiety and stress. It makes me question just *how much* pain is out there? How much emotional and spiritual pain is routinely covered over with a smile and a handshake?

If 19 people spoke up at that meeting, then there were probably at least that many others still so chained to fear that they would not. If leaders struggle this much, what do you think happens among their followers?

What I am trying to communicate is that, "if you are wrestling with anxiety and/or depression you are not alone!" And, that I want to underscore that there is no reason for any feelings of shame or embarrassment.

Condemnation Helps No One!

If you suffer from anxiety or depression, and work with a doctor, you probably carry some scars inflicted by people who love you. There is a good chance that some well-meaning individual, or group, has condemned you for seeking help from medicine *instead* of God.

The reason I believe this is true is because of my own miserable track record. Until I hit the wall I wasn't exactly famous for empathy.

Until my breakdown I regularly piled guilt onto people if they were on medication for psychological illnesses. My opinion boiled down to my perception of a lack of spiritual discipline on the part of the hurting individual. It would take a walk on the dark side for me to understand what others suffered.

Oddly, during those years when I pressed people the hardest to get deeper into God's word, my own spiritual life had substantially 'dehydrated.' It digressed from the healthy *experiential* faith that I had known during my days as a student.

Years of studying and preaching the Bible had taken a toll—my faith moved from experiential life to intellectual knowledge. My walk with God degenerated into a doctrinal position—a formula for living. There was less life in my faith than I enjoyed as a seventeen-year-old. The result of formulaic Christianity was that I had little mercy, toward others, until I came apart emotionally. It is amazing how well pain generates empathy toward others.

Of course, I never tried to hurt anyone. I simply didn't understand the *reality* of other people's emotional and mental pain. I also possessed a very narrow mind. I always valued the choice between "One *or* the other," above the choice of, "One *and* the other."

Pray And Take The Medicine

In situations where both prayer and medicine are available, is it really a matter of either/or? Can't we seek help from two sources at the same time?

I once heard a wise man say that if you have a headache, "You should pray *and* take an aspirin." Actually, he said, "If you think it is God's will for you to have a headache after you pray then do nothing. But if you think it is not God's desire for you to have a headache, you should pray *and* take an aspirin." That is good advice. I think the same wisdom holds for stress related problems. You pray *and* you take the medicine.

I recently spoke with a man who has a chronic physical ailment—it is one that, left untreated, will eventually kill him. When he discovered that I am on long-term medication he scolded me. He bragged that he is holding out for healing and quit taking the drugs, which the doctor had said would save his life. He says he believes healing comes from Jesus, and only from Jesus. Therefore he quit the medicine. The problem is, he's still sick and growing sicker by the day. There is a place for medication and it is a valid place.

We'll talk more about the partnership of our spiritual life, medicines and other tools as we continue to progress through this short book. But first I want to discuss the difference between what I call 'chronic' and 'acute' anxiety.

3
CHRONIC & ACUTE ANXIETY

O God, listen to my cry! Hear my prayer! From the ends of the earth, I cry to you for help when my heart is overwhelmed. Lead me to the towering rock of safety, for you are my safe refuge, a fortress where my enemies cannot reach me. Let me live forever in your sanctuary, safe beneath the shelter of your wings!
Psalm 61:1-4 NLT

Anxiety has many causes. Some are spiritual. Some are simply the result of too much stress. Some may even be genetic.

Looking back I wonder about the possibility of anxiety being passed from one generation to another. I can identify anxiety as an ongoing problem throughout my life. I believe that I've known chronic anxiety, or "Generalized Anxiety Disorder," my entire life. Since I blew an emotional tire, I've discovered that several people in my extended family constantly struggled with anxiety and worry. It can't be coincidental that they were prescribed the same medication as I take today.

Chronic Anxiety

Anxiety has stuck to my family for a long time. It's presence may have spiritual ramifications, but there were circumstantial contributions as well.

My great-grandfather lost a large cattle ranch to the Great Depression. He was a strong man who eventually rebuilt his life and raised my father after his parents divorced. As a child I loved to hear his stories about his forebears and the Oregon Trail. His colorful life included a stint as an old-time Western marshal. However, he lived in the grip of fear stemming from his Depression Era financial loss. For him, if it happened once it could always happen again.

When my dad turned fourteen he left his grandfather to live with his mother in Portland, Oregon. He moved from the countryside in order to attend a specialized (public) school in the big city. Upon arrival, he discovered that his mom had no room for him—the depression impoverished her to the point that she could not afford an apartment large enough to include him.

As a high school freshman, my dad found a job as a personal caretaker for a mentally ill man. On several occasions he awoke to find the man trying to strangle him. My father worked his way through high school with cardboard stuffed in the holes in his shoes. He would walk three miles, many Sunday afternoons, to stand on the corner in front of a friend's house. He always hoped the family would invite him in for a hot meal. Most Sundays they did not. Lack of money heaped of anxiety on my dad during the days when he should have been playing sports, or just being a kid. That anxiety never left him.

In my family, anxiety hung in the air like fog over the ocean. My father worried about money until the day he died. That worry found its way into my own head.

You might ask, "Is this a spiritual matter or purely a product of environment?" "Is it possible that anxiety is inscribed on the chain of a person's DNA?" Or, "is it a matter of a satanic assault against a family?" I don't know the answers to those questions. Looking back, I do see that I have been prone to *unreasonable* worry all my life.

I call that low-grade worry, "chronic anxiety." The doctors use fancier terms but this one works for me. It means that you live your life as if every day is a cloudy day (By the

way cloudy days do make things worse, and growing up in Oregon you get lots of them).

Acute Anxiety

Acute anxiety is when you 'pop,' as I did a couple of times when my problems got the best of me. It first happened during my freshman year at college.

Leaving rainy Oregon for sunny Southern California turned life into a party until first semester mid-term exams threatened to de-rail my train. One evening I realized that I had grown into a lazy student who might well flunk out of a fairly easy college. I came apart emotionally and hardly slept that night. In a day or so, I managed to pull myself together and got through the mid-terms in pretty good shape. After that I doubled down on my studies and got good grades for the rest of my college years.

Later, as a youth-pastor in a small church I developed fears that I would lose my job to one of my friends.

This guy was really sharp and he hit it off extremely well with my boss, the senior pastor. He was in love with a girl in our church and would come to visit her as often as he could. Every time he came around I walked about with a lump in my throat and pain in my stomach.

I never resented my friend, but I sure feared his presence. I doubt that there was any real basis for my fear. My pastor was an integrous man. He never threw me over for my friend. The problem rested squarely between my two ears. I was a chronic worrier just looking for something suitable as an attachment to my anxiety. When my friend showed up the anxiety flared into an acute state.

Chewing Your Cud

Doctor's call chronic anxiety 'rumination.' You got it—ruminating is what cows do when they chew their cud, or regurgitate and re-chew their food. People who are prone to anxiety awaken each morning to mild anxiety then spend all day looking for some reason to justify their feelings. It causes them to distort events and circumstances. They bend reality to fit their own false sense that something is wrong, or worse than it is.

Here are some ways chronic anxiety worked in my life. As a young pastor I learned that you can worry over church finances. You can become frightened of controlling people who contest others for leadership. You can fear that you offended someone because they didn't show up in church for a couple of weeks. There are lots of opportunities for a pastor to 'invest' their anxious feelings.

I got so good at worrying that I would spend most of my days off from work quoting scriptures, or singing reassuring spiritual songs in an attempt to unearth a measure of peace. Prayer, scripture and spiritual songs are fundamental to our lives, but sometimes we need something more.

When chronic anxiety flowers it blossoms into acute anxiety. This is when people can't sleep, become extremely short tempered or find themselves unable to concentrate well enough to keep their jobs. I don't know how bad it gets for you. I do know this—there are things you can do to manage your anxiety.

I am sure that a few good tools will help you control anxiety in all but life's most stressful moments. You can, and will, live a happy and normal life. Read on and we'll look at some devices that will work for you.

4

OPEN UP ABOUT YOUR PROBLEM

*Be happy with those who are happy, and
weep with those who weep.*
Romans 12:15 NLT

Shame loves shadows. We need to learn to let
the sun shine on our anxiety by sharing our
struggle with others.

Those pastors I mentioned at that
conference found a measure of freedom in
the simple act of sharing with someone that
struggled with the same problem as they did.

When it became permissible to *talk* about medicating their stressful lives, the anxiety level visibly fell. I watched anxiety drain from faces as people revealed the secrets that had held them in bondage for so long.

Talking And Praying

Talking and praying about our problems is incredibly powerful. Jesus said the greatest commandment is to love God and the second one is to love our neighbor as ourselves. One way this works is in the scripture that says,

> *Are any of you suffering hardships? You should pray. Are any of you happy? You should sing praises. Are any of you sick? You should call for the elders of the church to come and pray over you, anointing you with oil in the name of the Lord. Such a prayer offered in faith will heal the sick, and the Lord will make you well. And if you have committed any sins, you will be forgiven. Confess your sins to each other and pray for each other so that you may be healed. The earnest prayer of a righteous*

person has great power and produces wonderful results. (James 5:13-16 NLT).

That scripture begins by addressing personal prayer over hardships. It moves on to confessing sins to others so we can be healed. Somewhere there *must* be a place for confessing, not only sins, but confessing your hardships as well. You open up to your friends so *they* can pray and you can be healed. Love for God and man intersect when you discard shame and unveil your problems.

Long after my anxiety peaked I began to experience nagging fears. They were un-focused in that there was nothing specific that frightened me. But there was a cloud over my head that I couldn't understand. I shared the problem with our church staff. They surrounded me and began to pray. One person spoke *to* 'fear,' telling it to leave. At that moment, I actually *felt* something lift off of me. However, I was still a little surprised when one of my friends spoke up. He said, "It left didn't it? I know it left because I could feel it blow past me as it left." If he hadn't said that I might have imagined that something lifted—his words were affirming.

Please notice that if I hadn't shared my pain no one would have gathered to pray and whatever plagued me would not have left. We need to be open about our problems with people we can trust.

Changes

I met a man about six weeks ago who switched church services because he heard that I speak about these problems. Our church has seven services each weekend which necessitates a team of preachers. This guy likes one of the other pastors better than me but he changed over to one of my services because of his struggle with anxiety and his hope that we could talk about it.

The first night we spoke he literally shook with fear. This was in spite of the fact that he knew he was in a safe place where he could freely reveal his problems. We talked at length, then I introduced him to a man on our

prayer team. The two of them now pray
together every weekend after service.

The guy is amazing. He changes a little
more each week. He says that he used to be so
anxious that he would hide behind a building
and melt into tears at work. This happened
three or four times a week. Now he's grown
brave enough to share his anxiety issues with
his unbelieving co-workers. He still won't go
to a doctor but his openness with others has
set him on a path toward healing.

Talking To A Doctor And A Pastor

A woman in our church was once one of
the biggest movers in the Honolulu business
community. Then she suffered a
panic/anxiety attack. It knocked her out! She
turned into a shell of a person and eventually
resigned from her high profile job.

Later she bounced back, just enough, to
land a role in government. But she soon left
that position due to nagging anxiety.

At this point she began talking about her
problems. She spoke with me and later with

her family physician, eventually meeting with a psychiatrist who helped her greatly. I think it is important to say that she started with her medical trek with the family physician because many problems can be treated at that level. If the family doctor can't help you can always 'graduate' to a psychiatrist as they are specifically trained for emotional problems.

This strong Christian woman had been trying to solve her problems by herself and it didn't work. As soon as she reached out for help she set off on the road to victory. Today she is controlling her anxiety and is once again a successful member of the business community. Her openness about her experience also benefits others.

Don't Forget Your Spouse

I've learned to talk freely with my wife about my struggle. She reads my emotions very well.

I still try to put a pretty face on my difficult days. She is quick to ask, "How are you doing?" which is code for "Are you struggling with anxiety?" When she 'catches' me faking a good day she actually releases me from some of the weight of my worries. The simple act of talking about anxiety or depression is a tool that offers an open door to freedom.

My wife is so good at 'reading' me that I take her along whenever I see my doctor (psychiatrist). I do that so she can 'tattle' on me if I have managed to kid myself about how well I am doing.

Cultivate A Friendship

I meet with a friend every Saturday morning at Starbucks. We're wired much alike. We read the same kinds of books and enjoy conversing about world events. We talk a lot about places where we would like to visit with our wives, and we discuss our religious views. We also manage to solve one or two of the world's major political problems every Saturday (If we could just get someone to listen to us...).

For me, the most important part of this relationship is that I have a friend who thinks like me. In other words I have a friend who I meet on equal terms.

I think of our time together as Jesus in our midst discipling the two of us. Our friendship has born fruit in the form of an extension of our church—a Sunday service in a movie theater 25 miles from our main campus. That was my friend's idea after he led someone to the Lord who lives in that part of town. The expansion of ministry is good, but the best part of our friendship is that I can be open about my doubts, fears and stress without fear of judgment. What I am trying to say is that if you don't have such a friend, find one or at least start praying that you do.

We were not meant to get through this life alone. It is true that no man is an island. We need each other. The scriptures are right when they describe the family of God in this way, "…if one member suffers, all the members suffer with it; or if one member is honored, all the members rejoice with it" (1

Corinthians 12:26 NKJV).

We are meant to suffer together and to rejoice together. However, if you choose to suffer in *silence* the others won't hurt enough to bring you any help. You must find someone to trust—someone to share the burden of your anxiety and its underlying causes.

5
TALK BACK TO YOUR DOCTOR

*But God hath chosen the foolish things of the
world to confound the wise; and God hath
chosen the weak things of the world to
confound the things which are mighty;*
1 Corinthians 1:27 KJV

Medical doctors come armed with some
pretty powerful tools. Their training is
extensive. However many are rushed, often
complaining that they are so busy practicing
medicine that they have little time to treat
patients.

I know a couple of doctors who stand out simply because they take time to listen, really listen, to their patients. Each drives their team a little nuts because they pay so little attention to the day's schedule. Patients often spend more time in their waiting rooms than they would like, but the payoff comes when the doctor takes time to listen to their thoughts about their own bodies and minds.

Doctors who have time to carefully listen to patients are increasingly rare. Hence we've grown used to letting our doctors diagnose our problems without very much input from the people who really know what's going on—us!

It Pays To Push Back

After initially giving me tranquilizers that worked, and still do, my family doctor tried two anti-depressants on me. He did it because though I was feeling well I had, once again, begun to have trouble sleeping. The purpose of the anti-depressants was to restore sound sleep.

Unfortunately, both medicines blew up in my face. The first one triggered *extreme* anxiety. The anti-anxiety pills worked until I started taking the anti-depressant. The first new drug knocked me over the edge with anxiety. I was worse off than when the whole horrible episode began.

When I complained my doctor gave me two weeks to withdraw then put me on another anti-depressant. That one caused me to lay half-awake and half-asleep for a few minutes each morning. I thought I was hallucinating. Those were terrifying experiences. As a result I lost confidence in my family doctor. The result was a meeting with a psychiatrist who helped in new ways.

First he announced that my family physician had done exactly the right thing when he put me on the tranquilizer. Then he explained that the anti-depressants cannot help me. I am allergic to them.

There are more than 200 'SSRI' drugs on the market. They are actually called "Selective Serotonin Re-uptake Inhibitors." It seems that our brains produce a hormone called Serotonin which helps put us to sleep. However some people absorb the hormone in a way that won't allow it to do its job—help us sleep. The next thing he taught is that if you are 'allergic' to one of these drugs you are allergic to all of them. They fall into five different classes. I'd already experienced two of the categories and my shrink offered to make me crazy three more times if I doubted his words. I declined the offer.

He eventually researched an antihistamine that induces sleep as a 'side-effect.' I've slept soundly every night since. The great thing about this particular medicine is that it is not addictive. I could quit any time I want. But then why would I want to quit it?

Overcoming Guilt

Early in my treatment someone invented a timed-release form of my particular tranquilizer. One pill would last 24 hours. This meant that instead of taking a pill every six hours I could just grab a pill with breakfast and be out the door.

My doctor was thrilled to break the four-pill-a-day cycle. He was concerned that I get enough sleep, and didn't like me waking at 3 AM to take a pill. But the 24-hour pill didn't work. Three days into the new medicine I was as nutty as before. I 'knew' that every one of my problems was a disaster in the making. This is characteristic of people who suffer from anxiety. They logically understand that the world is blowing up. The logic is usually flawless, while the basic assumptions are *not*. Most of what worries us never happens.

My wife and her friend finally convinced me that I wasn't thinking right and that the new pills were the problem. We then turned to the internet for information about the medicine. We discovered that some people don't metabolize the 24-hour pill. I am one of those people. I might as well have swallowed a pebble each morning.

When I called the psychiatrist he first argued with what I had read online. I felt guilty for disagreeing with him. I deeply respect this man, but the medicine wasn't working. He was sure the pill would work if I gave it enough time. When I pushed back, he quickly switched me back to the six-hour pill. I was fine in less than an hour.

You Must Talk

The moral to this little story is that you *must* talk back to your doctor. If something isn't working say so! A woman in our church was diagnosed with chronic anxiety and her doctor put her on a medicine that helped greatly. But it didn't help enough.

She would show up at church with a frightened, harried look about her. I begged her to ask the doctor to raise the dosage of whatever he was giving her. It took nearly six months to persuade her to challenge her doctor. She felt that doing so was disrespectful. When she finally did speak up, the doctor doubled her prescription. She is doing fine.

Doctors want to help, but they can't help without input from us. It's called "feedback," and is anything but disrespectful.

A Small Business And Its Customer

Think of your doctor as a business owner and yourself as their customer. Do this because that is *exactly* the relationship you have with your doctor. You are a customer and the customer deserves a listen. At the end of the day it's *your* body you are talking about.

One of my friends lives in another state. He grew overcome with anxiety while his wife was dying of cancer and his business was on the ropes.

He'd made an appointment with a psychiatrist when he called me. We spoke for two hours. Actually, I should say he 'interviewed' me for two hours while taking notes on the conversation. He was prepping for his first meeting with his new doctor.

Later that day the doctor suggested that they test an anti-depressant that *should* begin to work after "about" two weeks. He fired back that two weeks was 14 days too long. He told her that if he had to believe that treatment would take two weeks he would get about as far as his car before going into complete breakdown. He then brought out his notebook and asked for exactly the same meds as I get from my doctor.

His doctor asked him to describe my symptoms and medications from what he had written in his notebook. Much to her credit she listened to her patient.

She felt that my stuff wasn't exactly right for him but that it would calm him in the short term. By listening to her patient she was able to buy time. She got his anxiety under enough control that she could eventually prescribe other drugs that better suited him.

By the way, she never did go with the first drug she suggested. By listening to her patient she was able to find something better. My friend's doctor is a wise small business owner—she listens to her customers.

6
GOD DOESN'T GIVE POINTS FOR PAIN

Is there no medicine in Gilead? Is there no physician there? Why is there no healing for the wounds of my people?
Jeremiah 8:22 NLT

By now you probably think I am some kind of drug dealer. I'm not but doctors are. And they are usually good at it.

I've promised you an entire toolkit but I keep writing about meds. Well, here is a promise, "This is the last chapter about medicine."

We'll get on to the other tools in the rest of the book. But I've got to include this chapter because it applies to so many people.

A Half Dose Doesn't Help Much

I knew an elderly man who suffered from Parkinson's Disease. He slowly lost control of his hands and eventually lost even his ability to swallow. If that wasn't bad enough, the Parkinson's meds have a nasty side effect— they induce anxiety in normal people.

This man was a Christian with a strong bias against medicines that affect the brain (although those words exactly describe Parkinson's drugs). His doctor gave him a tranquilizer to tame the anxiety, which accompanies the Parkinson's medication. Because of his sense of integrity and distrust of drugs he would only take half the dosage of the tranquilizer. You guessed it—he lived for years with low-grade anxiety.

He spent his final days in the home of his daughter who was careful to give him his half dose at regular intervals while quietly mixing the rest of the tranquilizer in the food she prepared for him. She *tricked* him into taking the full dose of his medicine. The anxiety left and his last days were peaceful and filled with enjoyable conversation. Years of fear and anxiety melted away in the face of the prescribed dose of his medication.

No Points For Pain

Like that man, I am a pill-hater. As soon as my anxiety got under control I made the mistake made by so many others—"I feel well therefore I don't need the meds any longer."

In my case I had to wean myself off the meds. To quit them abruptly would trigger another panic/anxiety blowout.

It took several months to eliminate the medication from my system. I did it by halving my dose first in the morning. After two weeks I cut my early evening dose. Finally I cut back on the pill in the afternoon and then in the middle of the night. To do it right it was necessary to repeat the cycle each time I reduced the dosage. It took a couple of months, but I did it.

At first I could just take one pill instead of two. Then I began breaking them in two, taking a half pill every six hours. Finally I bought a pill-cutter and cut them into quarters. Hooray, I finally got off the medicine and thought I was doing great.

All was fine except for one thing. I took my wife to see the doctor. I wanted her to hear anything the doctor told me so she went to each appointment. This time was different. My wife had things to say to the doctor. She loves me enough that she "told on me."

It seems that I was fine five days a week but would spend my days off trying to decide what to do with the precious free time. At the end of a day nothing got accomplished but a lot of fretting over all the possibilities the day held. The problem with my wife is that she is both very observant and usually right. She was certainly right about this.

After hearing from my wife my doctor gave me some good advice, "God doesn't give points for pain. Go back on the pills, they are the weakest thing I could give you. Just think of them as the aspirin of this industry." I went back on the meds and am living a happy life.

Forgetting The "Off" Switch

It seems that when a person finally capitulates to panic/anxiety they have already suffered long-term *physical* damage to their mind. The brain somehow forgets that there is an "off button" to whatever mechanism produces adrenaline.

Adrenaline can be your friend—just ask all those caffeine addicts in your workplace. It helps sharpen our senses and energizes us in situations that require an extra boost to get us through. There is also the "fight or flight" aspect of adrenaline. When threatened, our bodies pump out extra adrenaline. The adrenaline boost gives us extra strength to fight against whatever threatens us, or run away fast. Adrenaline is useful stuff. But if the brain forgets to turn it off we end up living with unendurable stress.

Think of it this way. Your subconscious mind forgets where it mislaid the adrenaline switch. This is what causes panic/anxiety syndrome. Along comes a doctor with a pill that allows your conscious mind to hit the switch every time you take it. Your conscious mind can use the pill to do the job that your subconscious mind forgot. Life gets better as a result—so take the pills if your doctor prescribes them.

7

DRIVING IN THE SLOW LANE

Take my yoke upon you. Let me teach you,
because I am humble and gentle at heart,
and you will find rest for your souls.
Matthew 11:29 NLT

I promised you that I'd stop talking about medicines so here we go. It's time for some simple tools that will cost you nothing but a desire to beat your anxiety.

Some of the best advice I've ever received is simply, "Drive in the slow lane."

Good advice but something entirely foreign to me at the time.

Actually it was Dr. Archibald Hart who said this, on that day when I waved my pills in front of everyone. When I heard him speak I'd been treated satisfactorily by my doctor and had read several good books about anxiety. I had my nose in the Bible a lot more than usual. My prayer life was good and I was beginning to *experience* faith like I had as a very young person.

I pretty well thought I had things under control but Dr. Hart showed up with some practical advice that I never found in any of those books.

Drivers You Love To Hate

I was one of those drivers you love to hate. I never drove anywhere. I *raced* against everyone else on the highway. You may not have known it but we were racing and I was going to beat you.

I already drove in the slow lanes, but what I did wasn't what Dr. Hart had in mind.

I had discovered that I could make better time by weaving back and forth in the slow lanes of the freeway than by 'parking' in the fast lane. Of course there was this little problem of endangering others with my driving but I hardly thought of that.

Then there was the matter of someone cutting me off in traffic. I wasn't about to let that be the end of the story. I almost always found a way to get in front of them even if it took a mile or three to get ahead.

It Got Worse

Our early years as a family were spent in Southern California. Several times each year we volunteered at youth camps in the San Bernardino Mountains.

I couldn't get myself to drive to and from those camp trips without racing against every other driver on the road. The problem was that we traveled two lane mountain roads. This meant that the 'race' involved a lot of passing other cars on dangerous, winding roads. There would often be a mass of stone on one side of the road and a canyon on the other. The story gets uglier when you understand that I drove this way with my wife and children in the car.

Although I was a diligent Christ-follower I drove like the devil. I seemed to have completely forgotten that,

> ...*the Holy Spirit produces this kind of fruit in our lives: love, joy, peace, patience, kindness, goodness, faithfulness, gentleness, and self-control. There is no law against these things! (Galatians 5:22-23 NLT).*

That scripture goes on to describe life that lacks the fruit that the Holy Spirit produces,

> *Since we are living by the Spirit, let us follow the Spirit's leading in every part of our lives. Let us not become conceited, or provoke one another, or be jealous of one another... (Galatians 5:25-26 NLT).*

As a driver, the fruit of the Spirit was far from my thoughts. I drove jealously and constantly alert to overtake and even provoke other drivers. I fortunately never had or caused an accident during all those years. Actually, all my crazy driving only took a toll on *me*.

Anxiety In The Fast Lane

I should have caught on without help from Dr. Hart. During the months leading up to the panic/anxiety episode I remember growing fearful while driving. I was very much afraid that I was going to do something stupid and cause an accident. Yet I wasn't smart enough to link the fear to my horrid driving habits.

Since then I've learned to drive in the slow lane, quite literally. It is simply more peaceful.

On the freeway I pick one of the slower lanes, get into position and turn on the cruise control. I sometimes find myself driving five miles slower than the speed limit because that's what they do in the "slow lane club." Driving is now a far more relaxing experience.

Turning on the cruise control and turning up the music turns a long commute peaceful.

The Slow Lane For The Soul

We live life a lot faster than our grandparents did. Actually, we live a lot faster than we did just five years ago.

Our busy culture has pretty well lost any concept of a Sabbath, or day of rest. There are always unanswered emails and a million things to do around the house. A soccer mom in our town hauls two kids to as many as four or five sporting events on a weekend.

I once spoke with a prominent author who travels hundreds or even thousands of miles from home nearly every week of the year. He happily told me that he was in complete control of his time and spent at least a half-an-hour of quality time with his wife and kids in spite of his schedule. He was too busy to realize that he was too busy. That conversation occurred a long time ago. Need I tell you that he has little to do with his, now adult, children?

You can choose the slow lane in life by taking time to listen to music, reading books or just enjoying quiet conversation. Refusing to bring work home at night or simply learning to chew slowly enough to enjoy your food are other ways of living in the slow lane. I love to visit with people from countries where meals equal to time for conversation. Somehow I think they enjoy life more than we do.

There is anxiety in the fast lane, whether the fast lane of life or the one on the highway. Avoid it! Living fast will eventually override any pills the doctor can give you. Drive fast and you'll feel a jolt of adrenaline. Toss in a little road rage and you can ruin more than your day. Stray into the danger zone and you could kill someone.

There are many benefits to life in the slow lane. Patience in traffic actually spills over to the rest of your life. Savor the slow lane. You'll find it's good for your soul.

8
MULTITASKING MAKES US CRAZY

...I focus on this one thing: Forgetting the past and looking forward to what lies ahead, 14 I press on to reach the end of the race and receive the heavenly prize for which God, through Christ Jesus, is calling us.
Philippians 3:13-14 NLT

The incredible rise of communications technology has changed our lives in many ways.

Today we are more connected to other people than ever before.

Technology For Good And Bad

While technology can easily overwhelm you and keep you from living a peaceful life it also brings tremendous potential for good.

My brother recently began texting me. Soon we were in touch four or five times a day. Even though we live 3,000 miles apart, we're closer today than at any time since we were kids. I thank God for smartphones! But think of the volume of email you answer every day and compare that to the number of letters you dealt with a couple of decades ago. We are growing busier with each new technology.

When I was a kid we dreamed about Dick Tracy and his two-way wrist radio. Now we all carry powerful computers in our phones. Poor old Dick must be spinning in his grave somewhere in comicbookland.

Our tremendous new technologies also gave rise to a monster called, "multi-tasking." And that's not so good!

Multi-tasking: A False Promise

As the internet and other technologies penetrated our culture they urged us on towards greater productivity. The idea was that computers aided productivity and the internet, cell phones and email aided productivity even more. That is true. After that it seemed that if we could *combine* work on the computer with answering email while talking on the phone we would be even more productive—multi-tasking seems so beguiling. But it turned into a bummer. Today time-management books regularly document the tendency of multi-tasking to *reduce* productivity.

I can remember when I would write a sermon while answering email, talking on the phone and popping out an article for a blogsite—all at the same time. I'd simply bounce back and forth between tasks as ideas arose. One friend soon caught onto what I was doing. He probably scolded me a hundred times for answering email while we attempted to converse on the phone.

Multi-tasking needs to go the way of the horse and buggy. It generates gobs of adrenaline. It's an obsolete concept and never could keep up with focused thinking. Worse yet, multi-tasking makes us crazy—it foments anxiety.

As for focused thinking, it is much like driving in the slow lane. It's relaxing. I am learning to stick to one task at a time. And, I've discovered that I get more things done in a day than I ever did while trying to do five things at once.

When It's Unavoidable

But there are occasions when you cannot avoid multi-tasking. My teaching assignments take me all over the globe. I'm into six or seven intercontinental trips each year. I find myself strangely comforted as soon as I get past airport security and into the 'system.' I am equally *unnerved* when it comes to packing for the trip.

The problem is that packing unavoidably involves multi-tasking. You need to get the right clothes together—sometimes for both warm and cold weather. My current trip involves both freezing temperatures in Europe and the oppressive heat of equatorial Africa. Then you need to think about electronics. For me this involves a laptop, iPad, iPhone, Kindle and all the cords and batteries that go with them. Finally, my bags include everything from simple cold medicines to malaria pills.

The most hateful hours of my life are those spent packing. Sometimes I can do the whole thing in an hour. At other times the same process stretches to three or four hours. There is no difference in the process. The distinction is merely how I am reacting to multi-tasking on that particular day. Packing for my current trip took four hours.

I've learned to prepare ahead in order to cut back on multi-tasking. I Pack things in "kits." Cold weather, warm weather, meds and wires—I bundle them ahead of time.

But I can't do this with 100 percent success as I keep remembering something missing from one category while working on another. Packing forces me to try to concentrate on several things at one time. I hate it!

My only defense is to try to break complicated tasks into their various parts. I then try to remain focused on one part at a time. Doing so cuts back on multi-tasking and reduces adrenaline flow and anxiety.

I've discovered that you can defeat the monster by cutting it into little pieces. Try it! You'll find it makes life a lot easier.

9
AVOID CATASTROPHIC THINKNG

Give your entire attention to what God is doing right now, and don't get worked up about what may or may not happen tomorrow. God will help you deal with whatever hard things come up when the time comes.
Matthew 6:34 THE MESSAGE

My wife and I recently moved into a new home. The entire process involved several extraordinary miracles. Yet I had a tendency to panic *whenever* anything appeared to go wrong.

That tendency is called "catastrophic thinking." It means that you look at the circumstances, gather the available data and then logically project them to arrive at the *worst* conclusion possible. As I wrote earlier, anxious people are extremely good at this. Their logic is often flawless but their assumptions are faulty—such as forgetting that God plays a role in human affairs…

The Backstory

My sister and brother-in-law moved to a neighborhood across our island from where we lived for 29 years. The neighborhood is fairly new and the weather much drier than ours.

Ruby and I had considered the location a few years earlier. We rejected it, mostly because it lacked greenery and adequate infrastructure (most new subdivisions do). We settled into a condominium located on a lake in one of the greener towns on our side of the island.

Then we visited my sister and brother-in-law in their new home. We took another look at the maturing neighborhood and decided that we would like to live there.

A combination of recession and overbuilding made home prices very affordable in that area. We eventually sold our condo for enough to cover all costs including commissions. We retain a similar mortgage (at a lower interest rate) and also ended up with some cash in our pockets. We now own a single-family home that is considerably larger than the condominium we left. The house was the model home for the neighborhood and we were able to purchase the designer furnishings at a low price. This allowed us to bless other people with free furniture.

The dry air renders life much healthier for my wife who suffers from asthma. A whiff of cigarette smoke would send her reaching for her inhaler in our old neighborhood. She recently loaded her car with groceries at a store with smokers on both sides of her without a single cough. This is definitely the place for us.

The Miracles Begin

This story is even better than what I've told you so far. It has God's fingerprints all over it.

We visited a model home in June and fell in love with it. We put our name on the purchase list for the model, even though there were four families ahead of us.

We then almost immediately gave up on that home. We then spent one Sunday each month perusing open houses in nearby neighborhoods. Our goal was to eliminate neighborhoods we didn't like before settling into the actual process of finding a place to buy. The trouble was that we could find no neighborhood that we liked as well as the first place we visited. If we couldn't buy the model we would wait until we could get *something* in that neighborhood. Did I mention it is a new neighborhood and that no one is selling?

To make matters worse my travels are mostly in the springtime so we would need to wait until the following summer before putting our house on the market.

Then everything changed. We arrived home from vacation in late October. Weary from traveling halfway around the world (Israel to Hawaii), we managed to stay awake just long enough to open our mail.

Much to our surprise we found an unsolicited letter asking if we would be interested in selling our home. We went ballistic with excitement, as we had recently found a house that interested us. It was in a neighborhood, which was suitable, though not our favorite. Things only got better the next morning in church. Our realtor had another person wanting to buy into our location. We now had two buyers without ever trying to sell our place.

But there was a snag. We were due to 'tent' our building to kill termites that coming Tuesday which meant bagging all foodstuffs on Monday. A couple of dozen bags lying around would create quite a mess. Besides that we were still unpacking from the trip and re-packing to spend a couple of nights in a hotel while they tented our place.

We simply were not ready to show our home to perspective buyers. But both families were seasoned homeowners and able to overlook a mess while looking at the 'bones' of a home. They both visited our place on Monday afternoon just two days after our arrival from Israel.

On Thursday our realtor got a surprise call from the developer of the first neighborhood that we visited. They had sold their last lot and were now selling the model homes. The lady wanted to know if we were still interested in the model home as none of the people ahead of us could qualify for the purchase.

The following day, Friday, we had offers from both families that looked at our condo. A week later our place had sold and we signed papers to buy *the* model home in the neighborhood we liked best—including the furniture. It was a dream, come true and it took less than two weeks. The scripture isn't kidding when it speaks of,

> God, who is able, through his mighty power at work within us, to accomplish infinitely more than we might ask or think. (Ephesians 3:20 NLT).

That house represented far more than we would have dared to trust God to give to us.

Catastrophe Looms

The ink was hardly dry on the contracts when trouble raised its ugly head. Our buyers had most of their money tied up in an investment that would 'mature' two days *after* we needed to be moved into the new home. This would put us out of our house and unable to move into the new place for a several days. In other words we were going to have to find a place to store a house-full of furniture. And we would be forced to ask our long-suffering friends to move us twice.

We tried everything we thought possible. We applied for a "bridge loan" but found the process couldn't be completed until a week after we needed the money. We considered killing our retirement fund to get at the money but that would result in a huge tax bill.

Being a catastrophic thinker I was quite frustrated with my wife who kept saying, "The Lord will take care of us, he always has…"

Even our realtor and the builder of the new home were at wits end as to how we could complete the transaction without going homeless for a few days. Homeless wasn't a problem as Waikiki is filled with hotel rooms. Furniture storage, however, was a big deal. I wasn't a happy camper and no tranquilizer could convince me that things would work out. Even scripture reading didn't help as I 'knew' this problem was too big for God. Kind of an interesting observation for a guy who once wrote a book called, *Prayer: Dare To Ask*.

Then the circumstances completely reversed. A new development changed everything. Our buyers found that their financing wouldn't work if they didn't cash in their investment a week *before* our deal was to close. A single phone call from a person who knew nothing of our problem resolved the situation. Catastrophic thinking wasn't so bulletproof after all.

Between November first and January seventh we had sold, bought and moved into the nicest home either of us has ever imagined. And it all happened due to a *series* of miracles. If left on our own devices, we would have had to wait another six months to even ready our place for sale. God was definitely at work.

A Lesson To Re-learn

You would think the miraculous nature of all that I've just written would convince me that worry is seldom my friend.

However I recently endured another bout of catastrophic thinking. It all centered on the travels that bring me to the airplane seat where I am writing this paragraph.

The trip was in the making for over a year. The plan was to teach disciple-making and church multiplication in South Africa and Cote d'Ivoire (You may know this French-speaking country as "The Ivory Coast). Both are warm weather locations. My travels would have me overnight in frigid Europe on the way there and in cold Chicago on the return trip. My biggest problem seemed to be figuring out how to pack for extreme differences in weather.

One day, shortly before the trip, a friend in Hawaii asked me if I had my shots for Cote d'Ivoire. The country is in sub-Saharan Africa and hosts a number of tropical diseases there that can actually kill you. As a person who regularly travels to some pretty remote locations, I should have thought about immunization but did not.

The bad news was that no "travel clinic" in Honolulu could squeeze me in until after the trip was over. Even if they could, most of the shots take about six weeks before they actually immunize against infection.

The good news was that I had already been immunized against yellow fever and the most common other diseases. In fact, those particular shots are required before they will even issue a visa. Did, I just mention the word, 'visa?' Knowing that Americans don't need visas to visit South Africa, I had just assumed that I wouldn't need one to get into Cote d'Ivoire. I was wrong

It was only as I was researching the shots that I *discovered* the need for a visa. This was just twelve days before I was due to fly. I spent nearly a day filling out papers, finally sending my application and *passport*, via FedEx, to a company in Washington, D.C. They said they would walk my application through the Cote d'Ivoire embassy and return the passport and visa—hopefully in time for the trip.

This company is great to work with. I sent my package across the ocean and the continent on a Tuesday and by Thursday they emailed that they were processing it. Friday they emailed that it was now at the embassy. On Monday I got *no* email and went into panic mode, fretting all day long.

Tuesday got the better of me. I phoned the company to apologize for the rush and to explain my plight. FedEx doesn't do 'overnight' to Hawaii and I was going to miss my trip if they couldn't send my passport that very day.

Needless to say this problem could create a disaster. We would lose travel expenses on our end. The people in Africa would lose money they could ill-afford due to cancelled hotel rooms, etc. Worse, they would be let down by someone they trusted. I was pretty distraught, even imagining that I might lose some friends in this badly botched process.

I severely needed to re-learn that I *can* trust God in difficult situations. It is the same lesson I keep re-learning…

A Miracle Of Compassion

The receptionist I spoke with, at that company, was compassionate. She told me that they would have my passport and visa sometime that day and would do *their* best to get them to FedEx. At this point my immediate future was in the hands of someone I had never met. There was some comfort in the fact that she sounded nice on the phone.

That Tuesday afternoon brought two emails from the company in D.C. The first informed me that the visa had been approved. The second bore instructions as to how I might track my package while it was in the hands of FedEx. Upon closer inspection I found that someone I don't know (probably the receptionist), at a company I've never visited, stayed after work to get my stuff into the hands of FedEx.

The following day, Wednesday, my wife phoned me at work to inform me that FedEx sometimes *does* make overnight deliveries to Hawaii. The passport had arrived at our house a day early!

Catastrophic Thinking Buys Nothing But More Anxiety

People pre-disposed to anxiety are prone to catastrophic thinking. They are good at it and can develop a strong imagination toward the worst possible outcomes. I know because I excel at it.

However, all that catastrophic thinking buys you is more anxiety. You double up on your problems. In doing so, you eliminate faith from life's equation. And, you solve nothing in the process.

The only antidote I know for catastrophic thinking is faith in God. And faith comes from reading and believing scripture. The Bible says that, "…Before you trust, you have to listen. But unless Christ's Word is preached, there's nothing to listen to" (Romans 10:17 THE MESSAGE).

The word has been preached to you or you probably wouldn't be reading this book. It is available to you every day. The problem is that we often don't really believe what we read or hear. We need to 'listen' to the message—really listen. We're talking about listening to the very still small voice of God that repeats the message of scripture deep within our souls.

I've found that I listen best when I actually witness a miracle. My weak faith grows stronger each time I link God's miraculous acts to the promises of scripture.

I wish there was a shortcut here. One that would somehow get people like you and me to readily take God at his word without having to wade through life's problems long enough to see his miracles before we believe in them. Some people have the "gift of faith." I don't and you may not either. But Jesus said we only need faith the size of a small seed in order for it to grow into a large tree. For us this is a process—a learning process, if you will. My goal is to learn a little more each time I see God at work.

I'll devote an entire chapter to growing our faith through scripture. But for now let's just remember that catastrophic thinking doesn't help and faith in God most certainly does.

10
DON'T PARTNER WITH FEAR

*And I will ask the Father, and He will give you
another Comforter (Counselor, Helper,
Intercessor, Advocate, Strengthener, and
Standby), that He may remain with you forever
—The Spirit of Truth...*
John 14:16-17 THE AMPLIFIED BIBLE

The other day I overheard someone else's
conversation (Now, don't judge me for
eavesdropping, I simply *overheard* something
someone else said while minding my own
business in Starbucks). What they said had

merit and is worth repeating here, "Don't let fear be your business consultant…"

Fear As A Business Consultant

What the person said has a nice ring to it. It sounds so good that we might write it off as a great sounding platitude and simply forget it. But many people do operate as though fear is their business consultant. Or, worse yet, they allow it full-partnership in all of life's enterprises.

I know a man who suffered a divorce due to his spouse's infidelity. She "re-discovered" a high school boyfriend and left her husband just a few months into the marriage. My friend later married a beautiful woman then nearly lost her to fear. He was so afraid of losing her that they couldn't have an honest fight. Every marriage suffers a certain amount of conflict and getting through them in a healthy manner requires honesty.

But fear had its grimy fingers around the throat of honesty in this relationship. This guy couldn't get honest for fear of saying something that would cost him the marriage. When he finally broke the grip of fear (with a lot of help from a couple of trusted friends) he was able to gain his new wife's respect. Today they enjoy a wonderful life together.

Another person I know is constantly afraid of losing money to the stock market. It seems one of his grandparents lost everything during the Great Depression and he is fearful of repeating the process.

Meanwhile I know a woman who did lose everything in the stock market a decade ago. She even lost her husband's retirement stash. But she *trusted* God enough to get it all back, and much more. The last time I spoke with her she was gushing about how God, through the 'market' had made it possible to purchase a string of rental houses which will provide a comfortable retirement. She decided that fear had no room in her life or business plan. Fear is neither consultant nor partner to this woman. God is her partner through his Holy Spirit.

A Valuable Lesson

Today seminars and conferences for pastors are a dime-a-dozen. I get advertisements almost daily to learn what one famous person or another has discovered about, "How to grow a bigger church." But it wasn't always so.

Two weeks into my first pastorate I was fortunate to attend one of the *first* non-denominational pastor's conferences dealing with the subject of growing churches.

I was the youngest person ever to attend this conference and the earliest into a new pastorate. That was much to my advantage as the sponsoring pastor (of one of the nation's first mega-churches) took a personal interest in me.

He put one of his staff members on me. The guy took me to lunch in restaurants I could never afford. They invited me for private sessions with the Lead Pastor. He would challenge me to *never* allow fearful words to come out of my mouth. They even asked me back to speak at their conferences as our ministry began to grow.

It was the part about, "not speaking about fear," that did me the most good. As a result of those people, for a time, I simply would not say things like: "For fear of…," "I'm afraid that…," etc. I simply erased the word, "fear" from my vocabulary. Need I tell you that those were the glory years of our formulation as a movement?

During those years, I managed to reject fear as a business consultant. Instead, I learned to listen hard for the voice of God in all things.

Jesus once told a group of his followers, "…do not worry, saying, 'What shall we eat?' or 'What shall we drink?' or 'What shall we wear?' …For your heavenly Father knows that you need all these things. But seek first the kingdom of God and His righteousness, and all these things shall be added to you." (Matthew 6:31-33 *NKJV*).

The more I believed that scripture the more I relied on the Holy Spirit to show me how God had *already* supplied our needs—even though I might not be able to see his supplies at the time. That belief made the Holy Spirit my partner instead of fear.

The result was that we became innovative. Instead of erecting bigger buildings (no land available) our church opted for multiple services. This was back in the day when multiple church services were fairly rare. We did this because of our assumption that God had already met our need—our problem was simply to look at his provision through different eyes. Today we hold seven "Sunday morning services" each weekend and we are busy planning an eighth in a few months.

Adding more services required either a thoroughly exhausted pastor or a preaching team. Preaching teams teach more young people how to preach resulting in the birth of more new churches. Fear would have held us back while simple trust in a few Bible verses resulted in fruitful innovation. This particular innovation has helped launch more than 700 churches dotting the globe.

We wanted to start a college or "ministries institute" so long ago that no one would even consider accrediting it. Today it seems that every large church operates some type of school but in our formative days it was a "no-no." Believing that God had already given us all we needed to do our job, we simply mimicked Jesus and got busy discipling our staff and any potential leaders. We soon discovered that Jesus' approach is so inexpensive that even the smallest church can adequately train potential pastors. Again this belief that God really does *supply,* resulted in expansion of the kingdom of God.

A Lesson I Forgot

Sadly, I somehow 'unlearned' that lesson about fear over the years. As I grew older I began hearkening back to past failures whenever someone would generate a truly innovative idea. I began to allow fear to function as my business consultant.

Fortunately, the time of my panic/anxiety attack coincided with the hiring of several much younger staff members. For a time I hitchhiked on their faith. I had enough common sense to know that they were in better touch with their generation than I was. I also, somehow, sensed faith in them that helped me keep my mouth shut whenever the "F-word" (fear) was trying to grip my tongue.

Along with the jarring impact of the panic/anxiety experience and the confluence of our younger guys, I went on a spiritual sojourn that caused me to read more dozens of books about the Holy Spirit in just over a year. In that process I rediscovered life in the Spirit and was able to greatly strengthen my faith. There is more to say about that particular journey but I'll save it for a later chapter..

11
PROTECT YOUR SLEEP

It is no use for you to get up early and stay up late, working for a living. The Lord gives sleep to those he loves.
Psalm 127:2 NCV

Do you remember the days when people used to brag about how little sleep they needed? I do. And it made me feel guilty that I need eight or nine hours a night while some people seemed to get by on just four or five.

A lot of that talk went around during the incredible rise in technology that so overwhelmed us as the 20th Century turned into the 21st. We assumed that if we could build productivity into or lives we could somehow infuse more of it into our bodies—hence we could learn to function with less sleep.

Change For The Better

Well something has changed. These days we routinely read magazine articles encouraging us to get more rest. Doctors have their own TV shows and sometimes build an entire hour of programming around the need for sleep.

Pastors once again recognize the need for Sabbath and companies actually find ways to reward workers for taking their vacation days in a consecutive stretch instead of a day or two here and there.

Changing Habits Can Bring Rest

If you struggle with anxiety there is a good chance that you aren't getting enough sleep. There is also a good chance that you have turned to over-the-counter medications to get more rest. You may have even discovered that while alcohol will put you to sleep it will also bounce back on you. Drinking yourself to sleep will cause you to sleep well for a couple of hours and then spend the rest of the night fruitlessly rotating on your mattress while pushing at your pillow to get more comfort.

I've learned some simple tools for getting to sleep. But first a disclaimer—I take a prescription antihistamine, which has sleepiness as a side effect. Remember when I wrote that our brains somehow forget how to hit the off-button for adrenaline? Well my brain still struggles by thinking about projects that excite me—this book for instance. The medicine helps with that on/off button attached to my adrenal glands.

You can help protect your sleep by refusing to watch violent or exciting television shows before going to bed.

You can, in fact, ban television from your bedroom. That may seem like blasphemy, especially if you have just installed a nice wall-mounted flat-screen in the room where you sleep. But bedrooms are made for sleep and certain other activities. A television is simply an invader.

I like to read. Always have since I was a kid. During the same summer that I got rejected from Little League Baseball I discovered a thing called a 'bookmobile.' The library would actually send books into the park where I hung out all summer long. I'd get my limit of five books every other Thursday and have been a reader ever since.

But, here is my point about reading and sleep. I actually have little time for reading so I've learned to read myself to sleep. If I am reading a book for work I do it in the morning along with my devotions. But I've learned to love history books and non-violent novels. Sometimes I get in as many as 20 pages before catching 40 winks. Most often just four or five pages makes me drowsy. Try it and you'll find yourself falling off faster. You might even become better informed about the world.

I discovered another aid to sleep on one of my trips. I was in a place so remote that there was, quite literally, no light and no sound in my room. I slept wonderfully. It was such a strange experience that I talked about it for days. You notice that I just wrote, "I talked about it for days…" That's because it was several days before I realized that I could nearly duplicate the experience with an airline eye-mask and soft foam earplugs. They work really well for me.

Soft Sounds

When I travel I play sleep sounds softly during the night. I set the music-player on my phone to repeat and leave it playing the same track just loud enough to counter any extraneous sounds that might otherwise penetrate my earplugs. I've learned that conditioning myself to sleep with the sound of falling rain now makes it easier to sleep on airplanes. I'm writing this chapter on a very long trip. It would be shorter to simply fly around the planet. I've spent three of the last thirteen nights sleeping on planes. With the help of my medications and music, I sleep well and feel very little jetlag.

The alarm clock used to be my enemy. I'd set it only when I had an early-morning appointment. The rest of the time my body clock would do the job. Then I discovered that I could catch a better nap if I didn't lay there worrying if I'd awake in time for whatever else I had going. I've learned that the alarm clock is my friend. My body clock has failed just often enough for me to lose trust, which translates into a half-awakened condition while trying to sleep. Now I know I can turn over and go back to sleep because my trusty alarm is standing guard.

Take Your Day...OFF!

There was a time when I thought vacations, days off and evenings were meant for work at home. I've since learned that they are for spending time with your family. They are also meant for rest.

Think back to those Hebrew slaves that Moses led out of Egypt so many years ago. It must have been a little disheartening to learn that God required one day off work from every seven. Keeping the Sabbath would have been a huge matter of faith for them.

If you had spent your entire life working for someone else you would have been eager to exploit your newfound freedom in order to get your hands on whatever you thought you were due.

Now God, who set you free from slavery, comes along and demands that you surrender one of your precious workdays to him. It would take faith to believe that you could get ahead in six days faster than you could in seven. But that is what he promised

It's the same with us. God still asks for a Sabbath. And it still requires faith to give it to him. I've discovered that faith is pretty much the opposite of anxiety.

I normally get two days off each week. I've learned to do one of two things. Either I set aside one of those days for restful activities or I work around the house in the mornings and relax during the afternoon on both days. This is particularly important when we've just moved from one house to another and there are a million things to do.

I am giving God his Sabbath and I'm giving myself a break. A day of rest does wonders for an anxious soul.

Vacations That Truly Vacate

Again, much like days off, I had to learn that vacations are really for vacating your mind. They are all about relaxation.

It isn't enough if you just vacate your usual premises and get away to a new place. You need to actually rest on vacations. I used to write books, read books for my job or work on my house while vacating. Just ask my wife how much she enjoyed this...

I remember lugging one of the earliest 'portable' computers across the country. It weighed about 30 pounds and got me stopped at every airport security point along the way. They each wanted me to turn it on—I couldn't figure out if they thought it was a bomb or if they were simply curious about the unit.

These days I try not to work at home unless I've intentionally taken the time (with my wife in agreement) to do some project around the house. I write on airplanes during business trips but leave the computer behind on vacations. While vacationing, we like to get away from our house if possible because the change of environment helps take our minds off issues that fill them at home. For us vacations are about rest, reading and sightseeing. We really do try to "get away from it all."

I also try to take *all* the vacation days, which I am allotted. This is crucial at any time, but especially when you are involved in starting a new project. In business or church start-ups there is a tendency for people to skip vacations and work extra-long hours due to a sense of 'ownership' of the venture. When we launched our church in Hawaii it was nearly impossible to get our dedicated staff to take their vacations. This left them over-worked and over-stressed. I'd rather be working with clear-headed people. This caused us to create a vacation bonus that only becomes available if a person takes two thirds of their vacation days in a row, or a minimum of ten days if they've worked for us long enough to get several weeks off each year.

I've also discovered that a couple of three-day mini-vacations a year do wonders for the soul. I used to pull my kids out of school twice a year for a long weekend. One of them was pretty upset over the loss of "perfect attendance." But my wife and I felt that family time and rest were more important than perfect anything. By the way, that child, as an adult, is really into long weekends of pure rest and recreation.

The early Israelis were given the "Feast of Booths" by Moses under God's direction. They were to spend a week every autumn camped out in "booths" made of tree limbs. This was a form of thanksgiving and rest after harvest. It must have value as I was in Israel last autumn and they are still doing it.

Rest is good for the anxious. Actually, it's good for everybody. I love Jesus' words when he says,

> *What I'm trying to do here is get you to relax, not be so preoccupied with getting so you can respond to God's giving. (Luke 12:29-30 THE MESSAGE).*

Think about it: God wants you to relax and *think* about what he wants to give you. Those words lead us into our next chapter…

12
MEDITATE, PRAY & KEEP A JOURNAL

Blessed is the man who does not walk in the counsel of the wicked or stand in the way of sinners or sit in the seat of mockers. But his delight is in the law of the Lord, and on his law he meditates day and night. He is like a tree planted by streams of water, which yields its fruit in season and whose leaf does not wither. Whatever he does prospers.
Psalm 1:1-3 NIV

According to dictionary.com, to meditate is, "to engage in thought or contemplation;

reflect." You meditate on the Bible by reflecting on what it has to say about God and his love for you.

The word, meditation, has become controversial in some Christian circles. A sad thing has happened to many who follow Christ. They have lost a major source of blessing by surrendering meditation to New-Agers, Buddhists and Hindus.

In fact there may already be someone scribbling on the internet about how evil this book is because I encourage people to meditate. For that matter even you, dear reader, may be offended because I recommended taking medicine for anxiety relief—well maybe not, because if you *were* offended you wouldn't have gotten this far into the book.

Did you happen to read the words I quoted from Psalms at the beginning of this chapter? They offer a special blessing to people who *meditate* on God's law (the Bible).

The upshot of the entire passage is in the

last sentence. It tells us that meditating on the Bible will cause us to *prosper* in all that we do. I don't know about you, but I can get both arms around a promise like that one.

Start With The Bible

I try to start each day by reading God's word. That Psalm speaks of meditating on God's word—not general meditation. Actually, I am currently working my way through the Bible, chronologically. I use one of the plans that comes with the *"You Version"* of the Bible, which is a free app for smartphones. I find it so useful that I tell people without a smartphone, "Go buy one just to get your hands on this tool for spiritual growth."

The *You Version* Bible app is a gift to people everywhere from a big church in the Midwest. It is available in just about every principle language in the world and has many wonderful features. Because it is constantly upgraded they must be spending hundreds of thousands of dollars a year just to make out lives less anxious. I like that kind of generosity.

I've also downloaded a couple of other "daily devotionals." Their purpose is to sustain me whenever I am reading books like Leviticus or Numbers that don't do much for my spiritual life. I actually read the lists of instructions and a census of ancient Israel in Leviticus and Numbers but must confess that they aren't too inspirational. I won't name the devotional guides I've chosen here, as you are better off finding whatever suites you.

Pray More

Jesus once said,

You did not choose me; I chose you. And I gave you this work: to go and produce fruit, fruit that will last. Then the Father will give you anything you ask for in my name. (John 15:16 NCV).

God has chosen you. There is a purpose for your life and it belongs to him. A number of years ago Rick Warren wrote a great book called "The Purpose Driven Life." If you haven't read it you should. When you do, pay close attention to the first sentence…"It's not about you!"

We'd all be happier if we got that thought through our heads. Life is not about *me*, it's about *us*. And I am happier when I am more interested in God's plan for *us* than when I spend time worrying about me.

The promise Jesus made was that prayer is a kind of a blank check for people who live their lives intent on bearing 'fruit' for God. This can only mean that God will fully resource any individual who intends to live their life in a way that honors God among other people. He said, "He will give you anything you ask for in my name." It suggests we can ask God for anything that Jesus favors and he will give it to us. I like that, don't you?

Praying is important. After my horrid panic/anxiety attack I realized that I had lost ground spiritually over the years. I possessed more faith in my late teens than I did as a seasoned pastor. I had grown dependent on accumulated experience, knowledge and personal capabilities.

I decided to try to change the situation and have largely succeeded. One thing I did was pretty extreme. I read every book on the Holy Spirit, prayer or faith that I could get into my hands—in a year (I was pretty desperate).

Want to know what I learned from all those books? The answer is pretty simple, "Pray more!"

That's it, "Pray more!" At the end of the reading marathon I understood that while I went through all the motions of a prayer life I was still *very* dependent on my own life skills. And that wasn't working.

The reading exercise brought me back to a time in my teens when I would lock myself in the bathroom at home and pray while kneeling by the bathtub. I shared a room with my brother and wanted privacy when I prayed.

I had learned to link prayer to *meditation* on God's word through Ken Hyde, my High School Pastor. He taught us to read, pray, and journal our thoughts and prayers. During that time I found a scripture that really stuck with me. It is my favorite passage in the entire Bible. It says,

> *Take delight in the Lord, and he will give you your heart's desires. Commit everything you do to the Lord. Trust him, and he will help you. (Psalm 37:4-5 NLT).*

I could really get into that part about my heart's desire and God helping me. As it happened I had one really big desire and needed God's help pretty badly. I had fallen in love—with a car.

One day, at age 14, I stood on the sidewalk outside of church and watched a 20-year-old drive by in an English sports car (If you must know, it was a 1952 MG TD). The car was already old and pretty badly beaten but love is love and I simply had to have that car.

But there were several obstacles to that automotive piece of art becoming mine. First, I was only 14 and had no driver's license or regular job. Second, the guy driving it would probably move on to something better before I was old enough to purchase it. Third, and most important, my dad knew a thing or two about cars--such as that part of the MG body was made of wood and that the electrical systems in English cars were notable for their unreliability. My dad was the biggest obstacle.

Then I found the scripture I quoted above. To me it read, "Take delight in the Lord, and he will give you your '1952 MG.' Commit everything you do to the Lord. Trust him, and he will help you get that car."

I began seriously seeking God—spending time in his book, praying and doing whatever he seemed to ask of me. And it worked. God *tricked* me into a deeper walk with him through that old car.

I never told the guy with the car that I wanted it. He was six years older than me and I barely knew him. He did eventually buy something bigger and better, but he saved the car for me. He had somehow heard that I wanted it so he put it up on blocks in an old shed until I could afford to buy it. My dad relented to the point that he later restored an older MG of his own. I delighted in the Lord and got the MG of my heart. But in the process God got all of me. After my panic/anxiety attack I knew I needed to get back to where I was with God in those days.

Journaling Helps

Did I mention that our High School Pastor had us all reading scripture, praying and then *journaling* our thoughts and prayers? The particular journal he bought for us was a kind of corny tool. I actually disliked it, but it was effective for its *function* if not for its layout.

The Bible advises, "From the rising of the sun to its going down The Lord's name is to be praised." (Psalm 113:3 *NKJV*). Praising God for his past actions greatly strengthens your faith. Journaling is a tool for praising God for earlier miracles in your life.

I don't know about you but when I am under pressure I have a very short memory regarding past miracles. The act of recording the linkage between scriptural promises, prayers I've offered and miracles leaves me with an indelible record of those miracles. My journal is my primary tool for giving God the praise he deserves and helping lift my ugly spirits during difficult and anxious moments.

When I began linking the promises of scripture to my prayers in that journal my faith *immediately* grew stronger. Then I added a twist of my own. I would enter the date of my prayer the first time I prayed it. Later I would enter the date when God answered the prayer and write down how he answered it. My faith took gigantic leaps as I watched God fulfill his promises in my own life.

Today my journal is in my phone. An app designed as a "to-do list" serves the purpose. Whenever God answers a major prayer I move the entry from the "Prayer" category to the one titled, "Answered Prayer." And I note how the prayer was answered.

I've even gone so far as to go back and record the major miracles of my life. This includes a couple of times when I nearly died and it most certainly contains the stories, in this book, about purchasing our house and getting my visa for Cote d'Ivoire.

Here's the deal—whenever anxiety tries to bite me I get out those lists of answered prayers and miracles. I not only meditate on scripture I force myself to remember the times God has come through in spite of insurmountable odds. I read them out loud in order to reinforce them upon my mind. This process raises the "shield of faith to stop the fiery arrows of the devil" (Ephesians 6:16 *NLT*). Those fiery arrows are fears and anxious thoughts.

I can't tell you the number of times that reading my list of miracles has turned a bummer of a day into something healthy and productive. I can tell you that journaling can link the scriptures to answered prayer and that the resultant faith becomes a fortress against anxiety.

13
YOU CAN DEFEAT ANXIETY

And Moses said to the people, Do not be afraid. Stand still, and see the salvation of the Lord, which He will accomplish for you today
Exodus 14:13 NKJV

There are lots of other things you can do to control anxiety in your life. They can be as simple as cutting back on caffeine. My doctor told me to stay off the stuff but I am good for a cup of decaf every morning—after that I lay off. But caffeine isn't the only destructive element you need to deal with.

Establish Routine, Reduce Rush

Building routine into your life helps. I try to arrange my life around a seven-day schedule where each week overlays on the week before and the one coming after. Although every day is different from the other, each week is nearly identical to every other one. There is security in routine.

I've also learned that getting up 15 minutes earlier than I need to takes away lots of stress in the morning. I don't feel rushed around the house. My morning routine is calmer for it. I'm hardly ever in a hurry when I hit traffic. I even spend about 90 extra seconds just standing in the shower with hot water streaming over my head and shoulders—it's very relaxing, you should try it.

Exercise Regularly

My wife and I met while we were starving students. A date around a Coke was an expensive adventure for us.

The result of our tuition-induced poverty was a lot of long walks in the neighborhood. Walking availed us to long conversations and we became good friends before the romance set in. The friendship is paramount for us as are our walks.

We talk whether we're walking or not. But sometimes we don't walk. After a few days without the walks my wife will start asking, "How are you doing...?" That is her way of asking, "Are you feeling anxious?" The truth is that walking, or any other regular exercise, causes your body to absorb adrenaline and results in a better approach to your day.

You may not be into walking. That's fine. But you will be happier if you engage in exercise that works for you.

Solve Problems Quickly

Are you facing difficult situations? Build a system for getting past them quickly. I do this in four stages. First, try to define the problem, stripping it back to basic issues.

Second, identify the root cause(s). The third step is to list possible solutions—I like a yellow pad for this process as seeing the steps on paper tends to clarify issues. The fourth tool here is to simply decide which steps you can take to overcome the problem. A fifth phase to this is in order: sometimes you have to adjust my life around a problem that *won't* go away. I try to do that in a dismissive way, one that allows me to ignore the situation as much as possible without denying its existence.

Got a problem with another person? Work it out as quickly as possible. Jesus tells us how to do this. He first says to approach the person alone to work out your problems. If that doesn't work, you should bring a couple of other people into the discussion to establish points of truth. Should that fail, you take it to the church (assuming that he is a Christ-follower). Then,

> *If the person still refuses to listen, take your case to the church. Then if he or she won't*

accept the church's decision, treat that person as a pagan..." Matthew 18:17 NLT).

The final step is one of dismissal. You distance yourself, emotionally from that person. In other words, if someone keeps trying to hurt you stay out of hurting distance.

One way to dismiss a problem is through forgiveness. But what if the person doesn't want forgiveness? Well try forgiving anyway just so you can get the troublemaker out of your hair. If forgiveness doesn't work there is another tack you can take, "Bless those who persecute you. Don't curse them; pray that God will bless them" (Romans 12:14 *NLT*). Remember, blessing *can* include discipline. So pray that God will bless this person in a way that only he knows is best, and then you can stop worrying about them and their actions.

Whatever you do, don't let a difficult person control your own emotions. Your bad thoughts toward them only hurt you—they seem to manufacture anxiety.

Deal With Debt

Money worries are a huge source of anxiety. Try to eliminate all debt but your mortgage. That may mean driving an older car and owning a few less nice clothes. But, at the end of your life would you rather have lived with nice things or with peace of mind? Debt is a monster, but surprisingly easy to defeat with a few simple decisions mixed together with a couple of money management tricks.

Getting past financial worries can take a huge pile of anxiety off your shoulders. A friend and I wrote a book that could help you defeat debt. It is called, *"Your Money"* and is available through both brick-and-mortar bookstores and online booksellers. There are many books and a few good seminars aimed at helping you crawl out from under a load of debt. Find something that works for you.

Cut Back On The World's Ailments

I was a news junkie until I had my panic/anxiety experience. My wife tolerated my bad habit but later confessed that it gave *her* constant anxiety. I would switch between CNN, Fox and MSNBC by the hour. The TV was seldom on one station for more than three or four minutes if I had the remote in my hand. As I wrote earlier the panic attack broke off all television for a period. But when I got back into it I had developed an aversion to television news.

Today I get my news from the internet. I read from the LA Times, BBC and a local TV station website. Once in a while I'll peak at Al Jazerra just to see what other people think. This gives me a pretty balanced view of what goes on in the United States, Hawaii, Europe and the Middle East. I still get news, but only about 30 minutes of it a day and mostly in the calm of an early morning in my backyard.

Chew Your Food

I struggle with acid reflux problems and find that this is fairly common among anxiety sufferers. Reflux often keeps you awake at night causing you to feel tired and prone to anxiety the following day.

I used to think that the anxiety was *directly* related to acid reflux until one night when we went to dinner at a friend's house. This man is an excellent chef, a perfect gentleman and he is from Europe where they know how to enjoy food.

My friend actually chewing it. He said, "food is meant to be savored." He further lectured that swallowing too quickly both spoils the fun and results in stomach problems. Since that night I've slowed somewhat. I chew my food more thoroughly and experience less reflux. I've also discovered that eating fast is both a symptom, and a cause, of anxiety. As an anxious person I've always been in a hurry. The hurry was impacting my ability to digest, which resulted in poor sleep and more anxiety.

Random Tools

Does this chapter seem a little choppy to you? Well that's because it's intended to feel that way. Life usually comes at us as a series of random events.

As you live your life get used to *randomly* picking up tools that can help you control anxiety. It will never completely go away. You scolded me for eating so fast that I swallow food after barely wouldn't want to live with no anxious feelings. For instance, neighborhood walks are a great anxiety killer. However, if all anxiety ceased you might merrily find yourself out for a nighttime stroll in a dangerous neighborhood. Or you might casually step in front of an oncoming truck. Anxiety does have its useful side. The goal is never to end anxiety but to control it so it doesn't control you.

We need to learn to live our lives in a manner that causes us to remain *alert* to new tools for controlling anxiety. They may come through conversation, through reading or through prayer. They will often arrive spontaneously and randomly. When they do, grab onto them—you'll live a better life.

Conclusion

Anxiety didn't attach itself to you in a single moment. It grew over time. You acquired it through a sequence of events, or your reactions to those events.

Similarly, you won't defeat excess anxiety in a single moment. Learning to manage it is a process. Hopefully, this short book helps you to manage your anxiety. If just one idea reinforces you in this ongoing battle then your time reading it was well spent.

One thing you might do in order to gain a grip on some of the tools I've described is to simply go back to the beginning and re-read this book, right *now*! Repetition is a wonderful teacher, especially when dealing with an unrelenting problem.

As I said earlier, the goal of this book is not to relieve you of all anxiety. It is meant to give you some relief while you live in an anxious world. I hope that you can feel a little more comfortable with the use of medications as a result of what I've written. That you will

draw closer to God, the ultimate healer. I trust that you will find some of the other tools useful. And I pray that, by any and all means, you get a hand on that on/off switch controlling the flow of adrenaline to your body and brain.

SAMPLE CHAPTER
"SEVENTEEN STRESSBUSTERS"
(AVAILABLE SPRING 2013)

My friend Rick Warren wrote a wonderful book that starts out with this sentence, "It's not about you." He's right. Life is not about you, or me. We live best when we live for others.

But at some point, life *is* about you. It's all about you. Your life may ultimately be about others, but if you are not healthy you won't be able to make the world a better place. You need to take care of yourself before caring for others.

Preserve Your Strength

Please forgive me if this first chapter smacks of self-centered pop psychology. That's not really the intention. But you need to put *yourself* first. If you don't advance your own priorities you won't be much use to anyone else.

You must reduce stress if you hope to contribute significance to those around you.

A bad example might be the best illustration for this – I have a friend who supports two daughters in college; cares for her parents, who are both afflicted with dementia; and tries to maintain a high paying job in order to fund all of this. She has no time for herself. She lives in personal poverty. She's in emotional danger because she is running on empty. Stress killing her with kindness—the kindness she shows to others. And if she doesn't make some serious changes, she'll soon be useless to those dependent on her. She must break the unholy grip of stress if she expects to succeed.

Useful But Dangerous

Stress can be useful. It is a great reminder for us to abort some project or situation that threatens us. However, it can also be a killer.

A WebMD article says that 43 percent of all adults suffer adverse health issues due to stress. Over 75 percent of all visits to doctors are related to stress in some way. Stress costs American businesses more than $300 billion each year.

Stress triggers a host of negative reactions. These include heart palpitations, chest pain, frozen shoulder-syndrome, breathlessness, dry mouth, ulcers, loose bowels, headache, arthritis, memory loss, sleeplessness, loss of appetite, decreased sexual drive, anxiety and depression. Stress is even blamed for heart attacks and strokes.

Aside from physical ailments, undue stress is an underlying cause of divorce and broken relationships of all kinds. It can even speed the aging process in many of the same ways that excessive alcohol or tobacco break down the basic tissues in our bodies. In short, stress is an evil task-master.

Jesus said we should love our neighbor as ourselves. I assume this means that you *must* love yourself. God loves you, so why shouldn't you?

You can detach yourself from unnecessary stress. Even learn to let it roll off of you like water on a duck's back. A lot of the damage materializes when we *engage* stressors rather than avoid or ignore them. If you learn to avoid unnecessary stressors you will live a lot happier and, perhaps, a little longer. Stress is not a lot of fun...

Priorities Versus Priorities

The first stressbuster is a simply a new way to work with your priorities.

A few years back I was stopped cold by a friend of mine. He told me I should *stop* prioritizing my schedule.

That shook me up since he was a highly organized person. I couldn't imagine him living without priorities. But, he wasn't telling me to live without priorities. His plan was to schedule his priorities *instead of* prioritizing his schedule. This isn't just a play on words. His approach changed my life.

Instead of prioritizing you schedule you can learn to schedule *your* priorities. You decide what is important to you and build your schedule around that. If you and I are at all alike, you've probably spent much of your life building your daily life around whatever lands in your email box. Or, you simply shuffle from event to event which other people wedge into your calendar.

Control Your Calendar

I can remember the days before we had mobile phones. I carried a paper notebook with a calendar in the back of it. My friends would routinely look over my shoulder inserting their needs into my calendar.

A well-meaning friend might point to an empty space in my calendar and mutter, "You've got time there…lets meet then."

This was crucial because my priorities were centered on my roles as husband and father. In my mind, I had set aside certain days or evenings for family time each week. But my friends couldn't read my mind. They did however, seem to respect red marks in my calendar.

In order to stop good people from ruining my life I learned to begin the year by marking a red "X" through the blocks of time that were my own. I learned to pre-schedule time for my children, my wife and for hobbies and projects around the house.

As a pastor I got lots of phone calls on my day off. After a day when the phone rang more than 40 times we unlisted our phone number. That was another way of putting my family first.

I was, in effect, scheduling my priorities *rather than* prioritizing my schedule. The problem with prioritizing your schedule is that you let someone else dictate the bulk of your activity. You then work at manipulating their draw closer to God, the ultimate healer. I trust that you will find some of the other tools useful. And I pray that, by any and all means, you get a hand on that on/off switch controlling the flow of adrenaline to your body and brain.

Conclusion

Anxiety didn't attach itself to you in a single moment. It grew over time. You acquired it through a sequence of events, or your reactions to those events.

Similarly, you won't defeat excess anxiety in a single moment. Learning to manage it is a process. Hopefully, this short book helps you to manage your anxiety. If just one idea reinforces you in this ongoing battle then your time reading it was well spent.

One thing you might do in order to gain a grip on some of the tools I've described is to simply go back to the beginning and re-read this book, right *now*! Repetition is a wonderful teacher, especially when dealing with an unrelenting problem.

As I said earlier, the goal of this book is not to relieve you of all anxiety. It is meant to give you some relief while you live in an anxious world. I hope that you can feel a little more comfortable with the use of medications as a result of what I've written. That you will

SAMPLE CHAPTER
"SEVENTEEN STRESSBUSTERS"
(AVAILABLE SPRING 2013)

My friend Rick Warren wrote a wonderful book that starts out with this sentence, "It's not about you." He's right. Life is not about you, or me. We live best when we live for others.

But at some point, life *is* about you. It's all about you. Your life may ultimately be about others, but if you are not healthy you won't be able to make the world a better place. You need to take care of yourself before caring for others.

Preserve Your Strength

Please forgive me if this first chapter smacks of self-centered pop psychology. That's not really the intention. But you need to put *yourself* first. If you don't advance your own priorities you won't be much use to anyone else.

You must reduce stress if you hope to contribute significance to those around you.

A bad example might be the best illustration for this – I have a friend who supports two daughters in college; cares for her parents, who are both afflicted with dementia; and tries to maintain a high paying job in order to fund all of this. She has no time for herself. She lives in personal poverty. She's in emotional danger because she is running on empty. Stress killing her with kindness—the kindness she shows to others. And if she doesn't make some serious changes, she'll soon be useless to those dependent on her. She must break the unholy grip of stress if she expects to succeed.

Useful But Dangerous

Stress can be useful. It is a great reminder for us to abort some project or situation that threatens us. However, it can also be a killer.

A WebMD article says that 43 percent of all adults suffer adverse health issues due to stress. Over 75 percent of all visits to doctors are related to stress in some way. Stress costs American businesses more than $300 billion each year.

Stress triggers a host of negative reactions. These include heart palpitations, chest pain, frozen shoulder-syndrome, breathlessness, dry mouth, ulcers, loose bowels, headache, arthritis, memory loss, sleeplessness, loss of appetite, decreased sexual drive, anxiety and depression. Stress is even blamed for heart attacks and strokes.

Aside from physical ailments, undue stress is an underlying cause of divorce and broken relationships of all kinds. It can even speed the aging process in many of the same ways that excessive alcohol or tobacco break down the basic tissues in our bodies. In short, stress is an evil task-master.

Jesus said we should love our neighbor as ourselves. I assume this means that you *must* love yourself. God loves you, so why shouldn't you?

You can detach yourself from unnecessary stress. Even learn to let it roll off of you like water on a duck's back. A lot of the damage materializes when we *engage* stressors rather than avoid or ignore them. If you learn to avoid unnecessary stressors you will live a lot happier and, perhaps, a little longer. Stress is not a lot of fun…

Priorities Versus Priorities

The first stressbuster is a simply a new way to work with your priorities.

A few years back I was stopped cold by a friend of mine. He told me I should *stop* prioritizing my schedule.

That shook me up since he was a highly organized person. I couldn't imagine him living without priorities. But, he wasn't telling me to live without priorities. His plan was to schedule his priorities *instead of* prioritizing his schedule. This isn't just a play on words. His approach changed my life.

Instead of prioritizing you schedule you can learn to schedule *your* priorities. You decide what is important to you and build your schedule around that. If you and I are at all alike, you've probably spent much of your life building your daily life around whatever lands in your email box. Or, you simply shuffle from event to event which other people wedge into your calendar.

Control Your Calendar

I can remember the days before we had mobile phones. I carried a paper notebook with a calendar in the back of it. My friends would routinely look over my shoulder inserting their needs into my calendar.

A well-meaning friend might point to an empty space in my calendar and mutter, "You've got time there...lets meet then."

This was crucial because my priorities were centered on my roles as husband and father. In my mind, I had set aside certain days or evenings for family time each week. But my friends couldn't read my mind. They did however, seem to respect red marks in my calendar.

In order to stop good people from ruining my life I learned to begin the year by marking a red "X" through the blocks of time that were my own. I learned to pre-schedule time for my children, my wife and for hobbies and projects around the house.

As a pastor I got lots of phone calls on my day off. After a day when the phone rang more than 40 times we unlisted our phone number. That was another way of putting my family first.

I was, in effect, scheduling my priorities *rather than* prioritizing my schedule. The problem with prioritizing your schedule is that you let someone else dictate the bulk of your activity. You then work at manipulating their priorities into some semblance of life for yourself. It's a lousy existence.

It's far easier to schedule *your* priorities first. After that you prioritize the other stuff. This way you focus on those things that are important to you and not to others. I think I can hear you protesting that some things might not get done if you do this. You are right. Some things will go undone. But those will be the least important elements facing you. First things first!

This is a simple paradigm shift. But it could save your family, or even prevent a heart attack down the road.

ABOUT THE AUTHOR

Ralph Moore is founding pastor of Hope Chapel in Hermosa Beach, California and Hope Chapel Kaneohe Bay in Hawaii. Beginning with just 12 people, the Hope Chapel movement has planted more than 700 churches around the world. Ralph travels extensively, providing church leaders around the world with biblical tools for spreading the gospel and planting churches.

He and his wife Ruby, have two adult children, Carl and Kelly. Both of whom are active in ministry. While continuing as "Founding Pastor," he recently passed the baton to Carl who is now the "Lead Pastor" of the rapidly growing church.

Catch his blog at www.ralphmoorehawaii.com or connect at www.facebook.com/ralphmoorehawaii

BOOKS BY RALPH MOORE

Books That Sooth Your Soul

Seventeen Stress Busters

Prayer: Dare To Ask

Your Money

Let Go Of The Ring

Leadership Books

Making Disciples

How To Multiply Your Church

Starting A New Church